HOME BREAD MAKING GUIDE SIMPLIFIED

Everything You Need to Know About Making Bread at Home Easily!

Homemade Bread Making

Introduction

During the holidays is when a lot of people set out to make homemade bread. You inhale the freshly baked aroma coming from your oven in your kitchen. Making and baking bread can be healthy for you and it doesn't cost a lot for you to make it.

Once the dough bakes in the oven and is done, you won't want to wait until it cools off to eat it. Plus, you won't want to go back to the store to buy anymore.

Making bread is easy and once you get the hang of it, you'll want to keep doing it. There are different ways that you can make and bake bread. Some people prefer doing it from scratch. Others prefer using a bread maker.

In order to start making and baking the bread, here are the items that you would need to get started:

• Flour

• Yeast

• Water

• Large Bowl

- Sugar

- Fat

- Mixing spoon

- Pans to bake the bread in

Here is a little more information about the ingredients and actions that you'll have to take when you are getting ready to make the bread:

Ingredients

Using Yeast

The easiest type of yeast to use is active dry yeast. It should always be fresh, so make sure to look at the expiration date on the packets. Having and using fresh yeast is important because you want the bread that you make be fresh as well.

For the water, you must get the temperature just right. Water is used to make the yeast dissolve and added to a mixture of yeast and flour. In order to get the right water temperature, get a thermometer. The temperature is supposed to measure between 110 – 115 degrees after the yeast has dissolved in the water.

For a flour and yeast mixture, the temperature for the liquid must be between 120

– 130 degrees.

Adding Flour

In order for the finished product to have the right quality, you have to choose the right kind of flour. One of the best kinds of flour that will do your bread justice is bread flour. Bread flour can make the best kind of bread.

It has a high content of protein or gluten. Gluten is important because it can make your bread have a special texture. Gluten helps the dough to stretch in the form of a web. When the yeast ferments, air bubbles will try to emerge. Using gluten will trap them.

All-purpose flour can also be used to make the bread. Cake flour is not recommended because it doesn't contain a lot of protein. Your bread will not bake right due to the cake flour not being strong enough to deal with the gas pressure from the yeast.

With whole grain flours, there is not enough gluten to justify making a loaf of bread. You would have to include all-purpose flour or bread flour to provide it with structure.

Using Liquids

Depending on what type of liquid that is used in the dough will determine how it will come out. If you use water, the crust will be crisper and the bread will have more of a wheat taste to it. If you use cream or milk, the bread will have a richer taste and a fine texture.

Using cream or milk will cause the bread to brown quicker. There is more sugar and butterfat included in the dough. If orange juice is added, it will still be sweet and will help to kill the strong taste of the whole grain effect.

Fats

When you use shortening, oils or butter, the bread will have more flavor. It's not a good idea to use margarine or whipped butter because they have water. Water is also found in low fat items, so they are not good to use either. Your loaf of bread will not hold up very well.

Using Eggs

Your bread dough will have flavor when you add in the eggs. Eggs also give the dough richness and color. Eggs give your bread a nice taste.

Adding Salt

Whenever you make bread, you should always include salt. Salt helps with how the yeast is developed and the bread will not rise more than it's supposed to. The bread will also have a good flavor. Of course, there are some people who would prefer not to use salt. They can substitute it with items such as yogurt to help the bread to rise normally.

Using Toppings

You can use different kinds of toppings to change the bread crust. You can use an egg glaze with just the yolk and add seeds or nuts. When you use an egg yolk for the bread glaze, it will make the crust shiny. The crust will still be crisp and golden.

If you want the bread crust to be crisp and chewy instead, spray a little water on the dough during the baking process. If you want the bread crust to be soft, brush milk on the dough before baking it. You can also use butter to make a softer crust. These are some unique ways that you can experiment with bread crust.

Measuring Ingredients

Include enough water, milk or cream that is needed and heat it at the specified temperature. Scatter the yeast over the liquid and allow it to sit. This is to see if the yeast is fresh and active.

You will know if it is if it starts to rise and bubble. You will be able to measure and mix the remaining ingredients to make the dough.

Mixing Ingredients

Create a round and deep dent in the middle of the flour. Add the yeast, liquids and eggs. Beat all of them every well.

You can slowly add the remaining flour that will be used. When you get to the point where you can't stir with ease, you can stop. Put flour on your board or surface where you will work with the dough. Combine all of it into a ball. If you need more flour, add it so that that your fingers and hands don't stick to the dough.

Kneading Dough

Start kneading the dough by turning it over several times and removing unwanted particles. Fold it in half in your direction. Use the heels of your hands to push it away from you. Make a ¼ turn with the dough.

Keep doing this until your dough has been smoothed out and feels springy. The dough and your fingers should not be sticking to each other. Add enough flour so that the dough does not stick to the board or whatever surface you are working on.

Rising Of the Bread

Lightly grease the mixing bowl that you will use. You can use butter or shortening. Turn the kneaded dough into the bowl and make sure every part is greased. Greasing keeps the dough from drying out as it rises while it's baking. Use a clean cloth to cover it. Store it in a warm area. You can place it on an oven (gas or electric) and allow the dough to rise.

When the dough rises to double of what it was, press your fingers on the top of it. There should be an indentation when you are done pressing with your fingers.

Making Loaves

Make a fist and push the dough down in the center. To remove the air, the dough edges should be pulled in the depressed part and pushed down. Place it where the flour is spread out and turn it. Shape the dough according to the instructions.

You can use loaf tins to put the dough in. Make sure that they are thoroughly greased. Or if you want free form loaves, use a cookie sheet and it should also be greased. Cover the dough and watch it until it has risen to twice the size. Since the dough will have more yeast the second time that it rises, it won't take as long to do that..

Baking

Preheat the oven to the specified temperature. Put it in until you see a golden brown color on the outside. You will know that the bread is done when you tap it with one or two fingers and it has a hollow sound. Take the bread from the pans and place on a wire rack to cool. You can add more butter on the top for flavor and a softer crust.

How To Measure The Ingredients

Baking can be a fun thing to do, especially around the holidays. It's not difficult to make a loaf of bread, even if it's your first time doing so. Get all of your ingredients together. For a regular homemade loaf of bread, you will only need flour, water, (or milk) salt, yeast, sugar and butter or vegetable oil for the fat.

1. Since you will have wet (liquids) and dry ingredients, you will need measuring cups and spoons. You can also use a digital kitchen scale for dry ingredients.

2. Use a measuring spoon to measure the yeast and put it in a large bowl.

3. Turn on the water and feel it until it gets to room temperature. Having the water at room temperature is very important because the yeast will work better. Get a measuring cup and allow the exact measurement to the fill line. The water should be poured in the same bowl as the yeast. Stir the yeast and the water together.

4. Get the milk, sugar, salt and oil and mix them together. Put them in the bowl with the yeast mixture and stir.

5. Put the flour (whatever measurement the recipe calls for) lightly in a measuring cup using a spoon. Level off the capacity with a knife and get rid of any access. The flour should not be packed in.

6. Place one cup of flour at a time in the bowl. Knead the dough until it has a smooth texture. You can add additional flour to keep the bowl and the dough from sticking to each other.

It is important that the ingredients are measured exactly as instructed. If they are not measured correctly, your bread may not turn out right. It could rise too high or not rise enough. Or your bread may have a tough texture, being difficult to eat.

This comes from putting too much flour in the mixture. You can also have a loaf that is not sturdy enough to hold its own because you did not put enough flour in the mixture.

How To Measure Flour Correctly

Take a spoon to scoop out a little flour and put it in a measuring cup. Go over the limit and then level off the excess with a knife. Keep doing this for as many cups of flour that you need.

If you are meticulous and are looking for accuracy, use a digital kitchen scale to weigh the flour.

You will also get a more accurate result if you use the spoon instead of dipping the cup into the flour. Many people prefer the latter because it's easier and quicker for them. They feel that using a spoon would take too much time, especially if they are cooking other food items at the same time. Using the cup will make you use more flour than you need to. You can test it out for yourself.

Making Bread Flour

Bread flour can go a long way. In fact you will find that the results of your homemade bread will come out better by using it.

Measure how much all-purpose flour that you will need. Equal the amount of cups of white flour with the amount of wheat gluten, using tablespoons. Mix the flour and gluten together and you will have bread flour.

Beat the mixture with the other ingredients and continue to follow the recipe. Continue stirring as you put in one cup of flour at a time. Make sure the previous cup is thoroughly stirred in before you add the next one.

Hand knead the dough when it is gets firm. You will know when to do this when you stir the dough and it releases itself from the bowl.

Add more gluten and flour (all-purpose) in another bowl if you are adding more flour for kneading the dough. It will be easier for you to lightly spread the flour over the dough and work it in while you are kneading.

While you are doing this, use large bowls to prevent a floury mess on the work area.

Mixing The Ingredients And Making The Dough

When you're ready to mix the ingredients, you can use a glass measuring cup to put the liquids in. Make sure that the quantity that you need is accurate and not above the line.

Before you mix and combine anything, read over the recipe several times. You will need to know what to put in when it's time. The recipe will be familiar to you and you won't waste time trying to read the directions why mixing the ingredients.

Make sure that you have everything at your disposal. Once you start, having to look for something wastes time. Preheat the oven to the specified temperature.

Heat up the water for at least 60 seconds in the microwave. Test it to make sure it is at 110 degrees. Pour it in a bowl and add yeast and sugar. If you don't want to use sugar, then add honey instead. The yeast is required to be proofed. The mixture should sit (proof) for at least 10 minutes until you see foam.

During the proofing process, make sure you have measured the ingredients you plan to use. They should be at room temperature prior to mixing them together.

Put the yeast (already proofed) in a large bowl for mixing. Include milk, sugar (or honey), oil and salt. Measure the oil over the bowl, to include any excess drips.

You will need to add three cups of flour. Stir the flour along with the other ingredients together. Take your time and start out slow so that everything will mix together. Otherwise, you'll have flour and possibly other ingredients all over the place.

Keep mixing everything until it looks even and smooth. When it starts looking like dough, include another cup of flour with it. You can use an electric mixer to mix the flour with the dough.

Make sure it's on the slow speed. Otherwise, it won't mix well. After using the mixer, add another cup of flour. When it is well blended with the dough, cover it with a clean dish towel or plastic wrap.

Shaping The Dough

Before you bake the dough, it must be shaped. Once you have mixed everything together, let the dough sit in the bowl for at least 90 minutes so that it can rise.

Punch the dough down to get rid of air from the yeast. If you have children who like to help you cook, you can allow them to do this part for you. The hand has to be in a fist and goes around the bowl and punches down on the dough. Keep punching until the dough is not sticking to the bowl. Flour will help to keep the dough loose from the bowl.

Roll out the dough with a rolling pin. Make it into the shape of a rectangle that will be the width of the pan that you will use to bake it. Put the dough in a loaf pan. The pan should be greased prior to putting the dough in. Cover the pan with plastic wrap. This helps to keep the heat in as it has to rise again.

After the dough has been punched, the dough will need to rise again until it is double the original size. This time it should only take an hour.

Kneading Bread Dough

Kneading bread dough is easy to do. You have to employ your hands throughout the entire process. Kneading dough is a very important part of the bread making process. It helps the bread to rise and helps it to keep a fluffy texture. Kneading is done after you have made the dough and before the dough rises for the first time.

Select a table or counter area that is comfortable for you. This will help you not to strain your back. You should be able to stretch your arms far enough so that you can knead the dough and not having to bend over the table or counter area. When kneading the dough, you will use only the heels of your hands.

- Before you start, lightly cover your hands with flour to keep the dough from sticking on them. In fact, you should have a cup of flour near you; this is to keep the dough from sticking anywhere else in your work area.

- To keep the flour from getting on your clothes, wear an apron. Or you can wear old clothes that you wouldn't wear out in public.

- Take the heels of your hand and push in a downward motion on the dough.

- The dough should be folded in half.

- After you have turned the dough to a 45 degree angle, use the heels of your hand to knead it again.

- Keep on kneading. Fold, and then turn the dough for however long you are supposed to. You can stop when you get the right consistency for it.

Greasing The Bread Pan

It is important that the bread pan is greased properly. You must have enough to go around because you want to be able to easily remove the finished product without struggling.

You can use butter, cooking oil or shortening to grease the loaf pan that you're using for the bread. You can even add a little bit of cornmeal (coarse) to make things easier for you.

Whatever you are using spread it evenly on the sides and the bottom of the loaf pan with your fingers. If you don't want to get your fingers too greasy, take a paper towel and fold it for you to use.

However, if you are using butter, don't use clumps and leave them in the pan. Back in the day, many mothers used the butter or margarine wrappers to grease the pan.

When placing the cornmeal in the pan, turn it so that every area is accounted for. After the bread is done, you just turn the pan over and the bread should fall out easily.

Baking Bread Without A Loaf Pan

Did you know that you can make bread without having to use a loaf pan? That can be done. However, since so many people are used to making bread with a loaf pan, they could not see beyond that possibility.

You can use casserole dishes or pots and pans that you may have in the kitchen cabinet. You can also use coffee tin cans to bake the bread in. If you go this route, remove all paper labels and any remaining glue.

Get everything together and make the dough. Let it rise and split the dough by how large the dish or can is. As you are cutting the dough, don't fill the can or dish completely. You want to have enough space for the dough to rise, so there should not be any more than one-third of the dough in the container.

Before you put the dough in, grease the insides of the dish or can. Allow it to rise to twice the previous size and bake it. When it's done, take the bread out of the dish or can. Allow it to cool on a wire rack for a few minutes and then slice it.

Tin coffee cans and vegetable cans are ideal if you want to make round loaves. Round loaves can be used for sandwiches.

If you are baking bread using a can or terra-cotta pots, the maximum oven temperature should be no more than 350 degrees.

Freezing The Dough

If you have dough that you are not going to use right away, then you can freeze it for another time. The yeast should be active; otherwise the dough won't freeze well. Add warm water with the yeast. Let the dough rise one time only.

After it has risen, punch down the dough. Then roll it out and shape it. It does not have to be shaped as a loaf. You can also make individual rolls or whatever you want.

Place the dough in the freezer as soon as you're done. If they are loaves, spray some non-stick spray in a bread pan. Place the dough in the pan. The dough will rise after you've placed it in the freezer. If you don't want to use a pan, use a cookie sheet.

For rolls, place them on a cookie sheet and place them in the freezer. The dough rolls should be spaced at least two inches from each other.

Make sure to label them so that you know what it is. When you want to use the dough, remove it from the freezer. Put the bread in a pan or a cookie sheet. Allow the dough to thaw out in a warm area where there is no draft. You do not have to punch down the dough again after it has frozen.

If you have a few issues with this, such as the bread is not rising the right way after you have removed it from the freezer:

- The yeast did not start first

- The dough rose too much prior to being in the freezer

- The dough did not thaw completely

- The dough did not rise completely

- The yeast is inactive

You will have to make some corrections. Inactive yeast should be replaced with new yeast. The dough should be frozen right after rising and shaping. Or you can

use flour that contains higher gluten. You may need to add more gluten or more yeast than what is given in the recipe.

Tips For Choosing The Right Kind Of Bakeware

When you are making bread, you want to have the right kind of bakeware so that your bread will come out right. You don't have to get a lot; just a few pieces will suffice for now.

Here are some tips to make sure that you are purchasing the best quality bakeware for you:

Get separate pieces. You will be able to look at each one and check them out thoroughly. You will want to look for corrosion, cracks or other defects. If you find a defect, then you should not purchase it.

You want bakeware pieces that are heavy in weight. Heavy pieces will help your bread bake evenly and the bakeware will last longer.

There are different materials that bakeware can be manufactured from. Depending on what you are baking, is what you will want to use. There is metal bakeware, glass bakeware and ceramic bakeware. People will use these to bake their homemade bread.

You can't tell that the bakeware is of high quality just because it is costly. Some of the costlier brands will crack and corrode more easily than the cheaper ones. You'll want to look at more than one brand of bakeware before making your decision.

In addition to the above, visit different stores. Every store will not have the same price. You don't want to overspend on your purchase, but you don't want to under spend either. If you don't wish to go to a brick and mortar store, then you can shop online.

Loaf pans are what most people use for baking bread. Loaf pans are good to use because the keep the bread in the shape of a loaf, hence the name loaf pans. Many people have their own preferences of what kind of loaf pans they will use. However, each one is different in its own way, but still must be taken care of when not in use.

- Glass loaf pans – They are affordable and should be properly stored when not in use. Otherwise, the glass can chip.

- Metal loaf pans – Affordable, but do not last; you may end up buying more within a few month's time.

- Paper loaf pans – Used for breads that are given as gifts.

- Silicone loaf pans – Can be used by anyone; they can be stored in small areas.

- Stoneware – Can be costly; on the other side, they last for a long time.

Selecting A Bread Machine

If you don't want to make bread the old-fashioned way, you can purchase a bread machine. Having one can be easier on you because you would just put the ingredients in the machine until the bread is ready to come out.

There are different size loaves that a bread machine can make. It usually yields a 1, 11/2 and 2 lb. loaf. Look for a machine with a delay timer. This can help you if you are making bread for dinner or eating it for breakfast.

You can also use a bread machine for pizza dough or to make rolls. You can find one that will make the dough for you, but it won't' cook the dough.

If you are looking for convenience, look for a bread machine that tells you when you can add ingredients for bread making. This is very convenient and helpful if you want to add additional food items such as nuts and fruit.

If you need a bread machine that will keep your bread warm when it's finished baking, look for a bread maker that has a "keep warm" feature. You may want other features such as those for the bread crust, different types of bread, or bread cycles.

Thoroughly check out all of the features and benefits of the bread machine to make sure that it is for you. After all, you are looking for convenience.

How A Bread Machine Works

The first thing to do with the bread machine (besides turn it on) is to make sure the ingredients are measured correctly. Different bread machines use different amounts of ingredients.

There will be a certain order that the ingredients are placed. This is important because it helps the bread to rise to a certain height. If you do not go by the order of ingredients, the rising of the bread may be compromised.

Bread machines have different settings. Some have more than others. You will find settings for bread types and bread crusts. If you purchased a pricier machine, then you will have more settings and features to choose from. You will be able to experiment more with what kind of bread you want to make. If the machine is less costly, you won't have as many.

The mixer portion will mix all of the ingredients together with a bread hook. When the dough has come together, the mixer will stop.

The heaters inside of the machine will set the temperature for the ball of dough so it can rise. It may also take on the task of kneading the dough so that it will rise again.

After the dough has risen, the temperature inside of the heater increases enough to bake the bread. With each increased setting, the bread will bake at another temperature, along with the crust so that it can be crisp. After the bread has finished baking, the heaters inside of the machine will turn off automatically and the bread will start to cool off.

Twist and turn the pan to get the bread out of the machine. To get the bread off of the pan, turn it over. Remove the dough hook before you start slicing the bread.

Clean the pan with soap and water. Dry it off and place it back in the bread machine for the next time that you use it.

How To Slice Homemade Bread

The bread is done and now it is time to slice it so that everyone can have a piece. Some people are not fond of this part because they fear it may not come out the right way. You can't just tear the masterpiece apart, so you'll have to learn how to slice it.

Here are some tips for learning to slice your homemade bread the right way:

• Get a knife that is specifically made for bread cutting. The cutting portion should be sharp. It should also be a length to where it would cover the entire area so that it will cut properly.

• You can use knives that come with bread machines. They are specifically made to cut homemade bread.

• Before you take that first step, allow the bread to cool. If the bread is still warm and you are trying to cut it, it will be difficult for you to do. Allow the bread to cool for a few hours before you try to cut into slices.

• If this is your first time, you may want to invest in a bread cutting guide.

Check out different ones to see which one would work for you.

When you start cutting, do it as you were sawing wood, but don't put as much force as you would a real saw. Start slicing at the top and go to the bottom. Ensure that the bottom edge of the bread was included in the slicing. Don't take a slice if the bottom part has not been sliced through. You can tear the bread this way.

Other Bread Making Tips

There is a way that you can make your bread come out the way that you want every time. Here are some other bread making tips that you can use to make sure that your bread loaves come out right:

- You can use plain flour to make bread. However, it's better to use flour that has a better and higher grade. It should also contain more gluten. Gluten helps the dough to me more flexible and stretch more. Wheat gluten can be found in many grocery stores.

- Go by the instructions as to how much flour you will need for your bread.

Depending on the texture and other factors, you may need more or less.

- Wheat flour that is coarse does not have a lot of gluten in it. The bread will take longer to rise and the loaf will be dense. Cake flour does not have a lot of gluten in it, either. The bread's texture will be finer and the result will be crumbly. This kind of flour should not be used when making bread.

- Bread flour has plenty of gluten and is recommended to be used when making bread. All purpose flour can be used to make bread.

- The quality of your homemade bread will improve if you use yeast that has improvers instead of the plain yeast.

- Kneading dough is an important part of the bread making process that should not be overlooked. Do it for at least ten minutes until the dough is springy. The more you work on the dough, the more spring it will have in it. You also have to factor in the texture when you are doing this.

- If there are bubbles of gas that are trapped inside of the dough, the bread will be light and fluffy. These bubbles come when the bread is rising. When the dough rises for the first time, allow it to double up. Only punch it down afterwards. It will double again after it has been shaped.

- If you want to add flavor to the crust, you can use a glaze over it. If you want a shiny crust, use egg white and water. If you want a dark crust, use egg yolk and water. If you want a shiny and soft crust, use milk. You can also use different toppings, such as sesame seeds or cornmeal.

- One thing that is common when cooking bread is that it is does not get cooked thoroughly. If the bread is undercooked, you will know because it will turn out looking doughy and gooey.

- When you bake the bread, use a pan of hot water and place it on the bottom rack. This will help the crust to take shape. You will know it is ready if the crust is hollow when you tap it.

- Also, tap the bottom to make sure it sounds hollow. If both of these are intact, then you are ready to take the bread out of the oven. Allow it to cool for a few hours before slicing.

- Water is an important factor when you are making your bread. The temperature should be 98 degrees Fahrenheit. It cannot be too hot or too cold. It's better if you use a thermometer so you will get it at the right point.

- Make sure that you measure the ingredients correctly. Any slight difference can cause a change in the way that the bread will come out.

- When the dough has doubled in size, it is ready to cook. You will know this by pressing your finger on the dough to make a dent. If the dent does not disappear, then it's ready to cook.

- Dried yeast is better and easier to use when you are making bread.

- The oven should be set at 220 degrees Celsius. If you want your crust to be crispy, place a bowl of water along with it.

- The fresher the ingredients are, the better the bread will turn out.

- The ingredients should be at room temperature when you use them in order to get the best results for your homemade bread.

- Use a spoon instead to remove the flour from the container and put into a measuring cup. Do not tap the cup to make room for more flour. Use a knife or flat object to level it.

- Use the directions on the recipe for preheating and baking the bread.

- In order to get the bread just right, use an oven thermometer. An oven thermometer will help you to be more accurate.

- If you are using more than one baking pan, keep them several inches apart from each other on the oven rack.

- You can tear the bread crust if you try to cut the loaf right after it comes out of the oven.

- You can have leftover dough to freeze and shape at a later time.

- You can keep leftover dough in the freezer for about a month. When you are thawing it, put it in the refrigerator and let it sit overnight. Take it out the next day and unwrap part of it. Allow the dough to sit at room temperature.

- For best results, place the dough that you are freezing in aluminum foil or a plastic bag.

- Since there are no preservatives in homemade bread, the loaves should be frozen within three days and used within the next few months.

- Bread can be reheated in an conventional oven at 350 degrees Fahrenheit.

A whole loaf can be wrapped in aluminum foil. Or it can be unwrapped while the oven is preheating for no more than 20 minutes. Slice bread and rolls should be wrapped prior to reheating.

- The microwave can also be used to reheat breads. It only takes about 15 – 20 seconds to reheat bread, whether wrapped or not. If it stays in past that time, your bread will be chewy and hard. Then you will not be able to eat it.

- You can use dried herbs to give the bread a flavor. However, you should only use about a third of what you would use if they were fresh herbs

- Be careful of how much cinnamon or garlic you use. Using too much cinnamon can mess up the structure of the dough. The bread may not rise to the size that it should be and the texture of the bread may be compromised. The garlic may interfere with the activity of the yeast, which is important for the bread to rise.

- You can use fruits; however if they are juicy, add flour to the dough so that you won't have a gooey texture.

- Be careful of how much fresh vegetables you put in the bread. Some of the weight from the vegetables is water, so you will have to make adjustments.

- You can also stir the yeast in the flour mixture instead of proofing it. If you do this, make sure to use warm water.

- If you are making sweet bread or other flavored bread, please follow the instructions for shaping. They will be different than what you would use for shaping regular dough.

Conclusion

Making homemade bread has been going on for centuries. Nowadays, it has become a staple, especially the holidays. There's nothing more appealing than the smell and taste of homemade bread. Maybe your mother has some old recipes that she uses. Some will make homemade rolls instead of bread loaves, which is just as good. Whatever you do, make sure that your bread making experience is a memorable one.

Maple Tree Books

If you want to get access to upcoming books on various topics, 'like' our Facebook page to be informed. We always offer the books for free for 5 days when they are first released. You can download them when they are free and benefit from them :)

Go to this website and enter your name and email to join our mailing list.

https://www.Facebook.com/mapletreebooks

And oh, dont forget to leave a review :)

Even if you did not benefit from this book at all we still want to hear from your feedback so we can improve in the future :)

Alternatively you can join our mailing list

http://www.MapleTreeBooks.com

You can join our Twitter page as well

https://Twitter.com/MapleTreeBooks1

Thanks for reading :)

We wish you success in this life and in the next.

Printed in the USA
CPSIA information can be obtained
at www.ICGtesting.com
LVHW091018031124
795564LV00007B/251